DIY Fascinators!

The Beginners' Guide
to Mastering the Art of Millinery
to Make Stylish Hats and
Headpieces

1st Edition

By Ashlee White

Table of Contents

Introduction

If you want to make your overall outfit standout in an instant, a fancy headpiece like the fascinators we're about to discuss will do the trick.

Fascinators are no longer exclusively worn by the royals or celebrities. Even ordinary people can wear them to any formal event. It has become so popular over the years not only among old people but also among the youngsters. You do not need a lot of jewelry if you have something fancy like a fascinator atop your head!

But just like most ordinary people, you do not want to spend hundreds of dollars buying a fascinator from a top designer, especially if you know you can make one yourself for just a few bucks. You are in luck because this book will tell you everything you need to know about fascinators and making one. You will find out the history of these quirky headpieces, who wore them and why. Of course, you should at least have an idea about where the headpiece came from before you actually wear one yourself, right?

Aside from these interesting facts about fascinators, there are also DIY projects that you can try at home using just a few materials that you can easily buy from any craft store or you probably already have at home. To make it easier for you, the book also contains a list of the basic materials and supplies that every beginning milliner should have. This book will be your guide in making different styles of fascinators that suit your every need.

Chapter 1:
What are fascinators?

You are probably one of the millions of people who watched the royal wedding of Prince William and Kate Middleton, Duke and Duchess of Cambridge. And of course, the wedding of Prince Harry and Meghan Markle, Duke and Duchess of Sussex. Maybe you even went to London to witness these historic events in person. Royal weddings have always been a fascinating event mainly because of the famous personalities. However, one of the things that people pay attention to is interesting headpieces that British women are fond of wearing—the fascinators.

What exactly is a fascinator? It is a specific style of millinery and is more decorative than functional. It has a large ornamental piece made of flowers, feathers, lace, crinoline or beads that is usually attached to a clip, headband or small comb. It is lightweight and does not give you a hat head and is usually placed on one side of the head. To learn more about fascinators, check out the next few paragraphs.

History of fascinators

So, when did people, specifically women, start to wear fascinators? If you go look back on ancient civilizations, you will see that women had always worn something decorative on their hair. Ancient Egyptians wore wigs adorned with gold. Native Americans decorated their headdresses with feathers. Ancient Greeks and Romans used jewels and fresh flowers, and even sprinkled gold powder, on their hair. The Aztecs added colorful fabric strips to their braids. Women in certain African tribes used leaves and pin their hairs with bones. The fashion of decorating one's hair had always been there. Maybe because ancient women felt it would be a shame to just leave the hair bare.

In the 13th century, women adorned their 'ramhorn' hairstyle with jewelled brooches. Imagine Princess Leia's hairstyle but bejewelled. The Renaissance era or the 16th century also witnessed the popularity of wearing headpieces like hats, hoods, and so on. These headdresses did not simply serve a practical purpose but also decorative because they are usually adorned with feathers, lace, or jewels. One famous wearer of a decorative headpiece is Mary Queen of Scots, who specifically wore *attifet,* a small heart-shaped cap made of lace embellished with pearls with one corner dipping over the forehead. In fact, the term 'milliner' was first used in mid-15th century to refer to products that are popular in Milan and neighboring regions such as straw hats, ribbons, and gloves. Those people who imported these products were called 'Milaners'.

But it was in the Baroque era, or the 17th century, when decorations for the head without the hat became a fashion trend among women. This was the time when trade with Africa was increased, which included ostrich feathers, making them readily available among the upper class. Near the end of the 17th century, the fashion trend called *fontange* became popular among women in the royal court in France, then later on became widespread in other parts of Europe. *Fontange* is a tall headdress structured with wire and covered with silk and lace.

Although the term 'milliner' was first coined in the 15th century, millinery as a profession was only established in 17th century. Milliners were often times women who specializes in decorating hats or hair to match the wearer's outfit, style, or even mood.

In the 18th century, women belonging to the nobility were often seen wearing *pouf au sentiments*, a decorative hairpiece adorned with jewelry, ostrich feathers, and even fruits. It was a way for women to express their moods and style.

Marie Antoinette, the famous wife of King Louis XVI wore an decorative headpiece during her husband's coronation as the new king of France. She was the one who started the trend among the upper-class women. She was known for her love for fashion and was even seen with something even more outrageous on her head such as miniature animals, landscape gardens, and a model of the French frigate la Belle-Poule.

You will see a drastic change in fashion in the 19th century, which values simplicity over extravagance. This was the period that witnessed global recessions, wars, and revolutions. And any hardships discourage people from wearing extreme fashion, such as the elaborate headpieces you will find in the previous centuries.

Before, only the nobility and upper classes followed fashion trends because they were the only ones who could afford to do so. But in the 19th century, fashion trends started to trickle down even to the lower classes in society. It can be attributed to the fact that the styles are now simpler and hence more affordable. However, it is still important to note that certain moderately elaborate decorative hats and headpieces are still worn only by the few fashionable elites.

Instead of expensive jewels, women now wear simple ornaments on their hair such as shells, ribbons, feathers, and cameos. Hairstyle has also become less fussy and simpler. During the Victorian era, hats and other kinds of headpieces from simple to extravagant are widely accepted in social functions. In the latter part of the century, small 'doll' hats that sit on top of the head became the inspiration for the fascinators and cocktail hats that you see women wear in the modern times. In the second half of the 19th century, American women have small shawls or light crocheted scarves worn over their head.

During the 20th century, simple hats and headpieces are now even more popular than their more extravagant counterparts. You will only see elaborate headpieces in royal events or other equally high profile social functions. During the popularity of the American flappers in the 1920s, women usually complete their bobbed hairstyle with a headband decorated with feathers, brooches, and gemstones.

Cocktail hats in the 1930s look a lot like the fascinators that we all know today. One popular wearer of cocktail hats during this period is Elsa Schiaparelli, who sometimes wore cocktail hats with something quirky like a full-sized shoe or a lobster.

In the 1950s, wearing a hat starts to lose its popularity and is no longer considered a fashion trend, except for the occasional cocktail hats worn on formal events and parties. People start to view wearing a hat as old-fashioned that only the elderly wear. The 'whimsy' was introduced by top French couturiers in the USA and UK and are worn by celebrities. It is a headpiece with a thin veil draped over the face and is gathered on top of the head with a flower or other decorative pieces.

Fascinators and cocktail hats became a thing again in the 1980s, when famous people like Grace Jones and Princess Diana start to wear them as statement pieces. Milliners Philip Treacy and Stephen Jones who are both based in London introduced the fascinators to the fashion elite and the trend took off once again. Treacy designed the headpiece worn by Isabella Blow on her wedding day. And Jones' shop boasts famous clients like celebrities and the royalty.

These days, fascinators are worn by women on special occasions and formal events, such as weddings, formal dinner parties, horse racing events, and catwalks. It is also now a trend to wear a wedding fascinator instead of the traditional wedding veil among brides. Royals are often seen wearing fascinators, thus increasing its popularity even more. Princess Beatrice and Eugenie attracted attention during Kate and William's wedding because of their fun and interesting fascinators. Once again, attention was brought to these headpieces that have become an integral part of fashion.

Why do women wear fascinators?

Some people might ask, what are the reasons why women choose to wear fascinators rather than proper hats. Fascinators can be customized according to the wearer's outfit, style, or mood.

This means that it is a great way to express yourself. If you are trying to channel your inner Marie Antoinette, you can wear something extravagant with ostrich feathers and jewels. If you just want to stand out, wear something different like a cage with a fake bird inside. It can be a fun way to dress up for a formal event. Some also wear fascinators to honor tradition, like the royals. Others just wear it because it instantly makes their simple outfit more formal and dressy.

What sets apart fascinators from other headpieces?

One important thing to take note of about fascinators is that it does not come with a hat and is usually made of feathers, crib, veil, and many different kinds of embellishments. It is purely a decorative piece that sits on one side or on top of the head. Milliners argue, however, that not everything that sits on one's head can be called a fascinator. People all over the world became so obsessed with what the guests were wearing on their heads during Kate and William's wedding that they start calling any fancy headpiece a fascinator.

When should one wear fascinators?

In these modern day when you are allowed to wear almost anything, you can wear fascinators anytime you want. However, they are most commonly worn in formal events like weddings, black tie events, red carpet events, dinner parties, and so on. In British weddings, the invitation will let you know if wearing a headpiece is "encouraged". However, it has become a part of tradition for women to wear something classy and chic on their head, which is why fascinators are very popular in weddings. You can also wear it at Kentucky Derby, garden or tea parties, and art opening.

Chapter 2:
How to Wear Fascinators

Since wearing a fascinator is not as simple as wearing a hat, you need to know some useful tips for wearing it the right way. It is not something that you just put on your head and be done with it. It is more complicated because of the many different materials and embellishments attached to the piece.

Choosing a fascinator

You need to consider a number of factors for wearing a fascinator. Although you can wear any kind of fascinator you want especially if you are wearing it for self-expression, you can still greatly benefit from following a set of guidelines. This is helpful for women who have not worn a fascinator before and are just starting to try this fashion trend.

Your hairstyle

The rule of thumb here is that the bigger and voluminous your hair, the bigger your fascinator. If you are sporting a pixie cut or your hair is slicked back, a small fascinator will look just fine. Medium-sized hairstyles call for a medium-sized fascinator. And you can get away with a large-sized fascinator if you are wearing your voluminous hair down.

Your hair color

Just like with choosing your clothes, your hair color also plays a big part when it comes to choosing what you are going to wear on your head. Brunettes or women with dark hair can get away with bright and deep shades like emerald green, pink, or red. Women with blonde hair can wear neutral colors like taupe or light warm colors like peach or coral. Redheads can wear a fascinator in deep green or earthy tones such as brown or beige.

Your face shape

The shape of your fascinator should not match the shape of your face. This means that if your face is on the longer or thinner side, avoid fascinators that are tall or elongated because it will make your face look even longer. Opt for a rounded or disc-shaped fascinator. Likewise, if you have a rounded face, avoid rounded fascinators and instead choose a tall fascinator that adds evens out the roundness of your face.

Your outfit

Your fascinator should complement what you are wearing in terms of color and style. Try to choose a fascinator that matches the color of your clothes to tie the whole look together. If your fascinator is made of different materials in different colors, your outfit should at least match the most dominant color in the fascinator. In terms of style, if you are already wearing a statement dress, wearing an extravagant looking fascinator might be a bit too much. Instead, opt for something a little simple and toned down. But if you are going for a costume-y look, then by all means wear the biggest and fanciest fascinator that you can get your hands on.

The season

Fascinators are made using different materials. If it is summer, you can find something made of lightweight material that allows air to circulate such as straw or netting. If it is winter, you can wear something made of thicker or heavier material such as felt or wool.

Others factors

If you are wearing glasses, you should not choose a fascinator attached to a headband since these are worn behind the ears and so are your glasses. It is also best to pick simple fascinators if you are wearing glasses because you do not want your head area to look 'too busy' with all the accessories. Or better yet, just ditch your glasses and wear contacts so that you can wear any kind of fascinators that you like without worrying about your glasses.

Securing a fascinator

Fascinators require special steps for securing one on your head. It is not as simple as placing it on top of your head, like wearing a hat. You need to follow certain instructions to ensure that the fascinator will stay in place during the event.

Wash your hair the day before you need to wear the fascinator

Do not wash your hair on the day itself. The idea behind this is that pins and clips have a better grip on dirty hair than newly washed hair. This means that your fascinator will less likely slip off your hair if your hair is a little dirty.

Comb your hair to the back

To do this, gather the section of your hair where you are going to put the fascinator and comb it backwards, making sure that the strokes are directed towards the center. Teasing your hair like this adds volume and knotting, which keeps the fascinator secured and in place.

Apply hairspray on your hair

After backcombing your hair, apply hairspray on the same hair section. This will ensure that the hair will retain its volume and structure.

Secure the fascinator on your head

If you are using a comb fascinator, push it firmly against your scalp. The direction of the comb should be towards the back of your head. Some fascinators use pins and clips, while others are attached to a headband. If you are wearing a fascinator secured by an elastic, you should wear it behind your ears and on the nape of your neck. Never wear it under your chin or you will look stupid. To add stability and security, you can choose a fascinator with a comb and also a headband. There are also fascinators that can be secured using elastic bands, although this is not really advisable especially if you just had your hair done and you do not want to ruin it.

Tips for wearing fascinators

You already know by now that there is a proper way to wear fascinators. You need to know these things before you go out wearing one on your head. These tips are especially helpful for first time wearers.

Wear it to the side

The most common way to wear a fascinator is by wearing it on either the left or right side of your head. Wear it just above your eyebrow. Some women wear it in the middle of their head, just above the forehead. This is also acceptable although you might feel a little awkward especially if this is your first time to wear a fascinator. Try this bolder look when you are already a confident wearer of fascinator.

Go for something traditional

If you are a first-time wearer, opt for a classic and traditional fascinator rather than going for something out of this world that might make you feel uncomfortable because people will definitely look at your headpiece.

Less is more

You might want to wear a fascinator that has everything--feathers, rhinestones, flowers, lace, and so on. However, it is best to opt for something simple, made of only a few different materials. Try to steer away from rhinestones specifically because it can look a little tacky if not done properly.

Wear it the whole day!

You do not need to worry about hat hair if you are wearing a fascinator. It is just like wearing an extravagant barrette. You can wear it from morning until the evening and your hair will look exactly the same, unlike if you are wearing a hat. You also do not need to find a place where you can put your hat every time you take it off your head. This can be a hassle especially if the event is the whole day.

Etiquette

Do not wear a fascinator to a theater, symphony, or any event where you will be sitting with people all around you out of courtesy. Those who are sitting behind you will not be able to see because your fascinator is blocking their view and those who are sitting beside you might find it a little annoying. Another important thing to consider is not to wear a tall fascinator if you are taller than your escort or date, unless you really want to emphasize your height difference.

Now that you have a general idea about fascinators and tips for wearing them, you now need to know how you can make one yourself. It would be nice to be able to create something that you can wear on a special event. Besides, formal headpieces can be pretty expensive, so making one yourself is also good for your budget.

Chapter 3:
Basic Millinery Tools
and Supplies

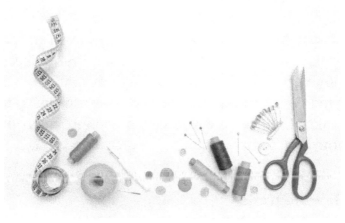

Although the art of making hats has been around for ages, the basic tools and supplies used in millinery remain more or less the same. Of course, there are now modern tools that makes certain tasks a lot easier but these are things that are not necessarily a must-have in your basic millinery supply kit. It is important that you have an idea of the things that you will need before you start your first project. It will save you a lot of time if you already know how to use the tools that you need to make a fascinator.

Some of the tools and supplies in this list may not be needed in the projects that you will find in this book, but at least you will have an idea in case you come across the same material in a different project in the future. Moreover, this list does not only apply to making fascinators but also hats and other types of headpieces in general. You do not need to buy all of them at once, or you will end up broke before you even begin your first project. What you can do is to buy the ones that you will need on the first project that you are going to make. Chances are you can use them again on your succeeding projects.

Sewing tools

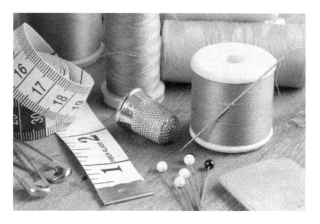

You will need basic sewing tools for making fascinators and other types of headpieces since you will be working with different kinds of fabric and similar materials that require sewing. This means you also need to have basic sewing skills (which you probably already have if you are interested in making fascinators). Some basic sewing skills that you need are needles, threads, scissors, thimble, tape measure, pins, tailor's chalk, and so on. You probably already have these at home, which means you do not really need to buy a new sewing kit.

Some projects may require special scissors. However, just buy these special scissors if the projects calls for one and you absolutely cannot proceed without it.

You will need both hand and machine sewing needles. You will do mostly hand sewing when it comes to making fascinators, especially if you are working on something small. There are different kinds of hand-sewing needles, but you will most likely use the ones that are a little bigger than the normal needles that you use for mending clothes. For instance, if you are working on felt or straw, you will need a slightly thicker needle. Basically, the thickness and length of your needle depends on the kind of material you are working with. It also largely depends on how comfortable you are handling the needle.

You may not need a sewing machine in most projects because the art of millinery requires a lot of hand sewing, but it is still a great idea to have a one on hand especially if you need to make several pieces and speed is an essential factor. It is acceptable to do machine sewing in areas that are hidden from view, or you can also use a sewing machine if the stitching is an important feature of the fascinator. It all depends on the project that you are doing. However, in millinery, you will be most likely required to sew by hand a lot of times so sewing machine is not exactly an essential equipment.

Aside from needles, thimbles are also a must-have for making fascinators especially if you are working with thick materials. Choose something that perfectly fits. If you have long fingernails, choose the kind that has an opening on both ends.

You will also need different kinds and colors of threads for your projects. It is best to choose high quality threads that will not snap easily when pulled. Low quality threads are those that are unevenly spun and are fluffy which makes them difficult to pull through the material.

A tape measure is another must have in hat making. You can use the regular one made of soft plastic or you can also find that special tape measure made of steel that allows you to measure the inside of a hat. This is something that you may be interested in buying if you decide to make hats.

But for fascinators, a simple tape measure, or even an ordinary ruler, will do.

Pins are used for temporarily securing pieces before sewing them with thread and tailor's chalk are used for marking fabric and other materials where you need to make a cut or stitches.

Wire cutters and pliers

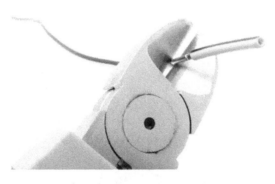

You will be working with hat wires when making fascinators. You can use pliers to bend wires in your desired shape or to make knots and twists. You also need a pair of wire cutters for trimming wires. You cannot simply use your hand for shaping the wires. Also, using a regular pair of scissors to cut wires may only cause damage. So be sure to use the right kind of material when working with wires. For the pliers, it is best to get yourself long nose pliers because these are versatile and make it easier for you to handle thin wires.

Millinery wire

Or simply called hat wires, are wires used for shaping hats and other headpieces. You can also use this for making decorative pieces for your fascinators. For instance, you can make your own leaf-shaped ornament using a wire and covering it with sinamay or fabric. For hat making purposes, it is best to choose hat wires that are covered with cotton because it makes it easier to sew the wires together. Plain wire or wire covered with paper is not enough especially if you want your hat to be sturdy and secure.

Fabric and other similar materials

You will need small pieces of fabric or other similar materials for making your fascinators. Some fascinators do not have a base but still requires fabric or similar materials like lace or ribbons. Other fascinators have a base, and for these you might need felt or straw. You will also need fabric for fascinators with a veil. Other similar materials that you might need for your projects are leather and special fabrics like sinamay, paris cloth, silk abaca, linen buntal, and jinsin, to name a few.

You can also use thermoplastics for your foundation or base., although they do not look as pretty as the natural fabrics.

Feathers and flowers

When you think of fascinators, you probably automatically imagine something with feathers or flowers. Everyone's general idea of fascinators is more or less accurate because feathers and flowers are popular decorative pieces in making not only fascinators but other headpieces as well. You already know that feathers have always been a feature of hats and fascinators. They have been worn by ladies hundreds of years ago. You can use ostrich feather (which is still the most popular choice), pheasant feather, guinea fowl wing feather, and so on. You can buy real feathers or you can also choose faux feathers if wearing something that comes from a real bird bothers you.

Aside from feathers, flowers are also popular decorative element in making fascinators. Silk flowers are commonly used for these hat making projects. These are simply flowers made of silk fabric, which instantly adds a luxurious feel to your fascinator. Aside from silk, you can also use other types of fabric such as velvet, which also looks luxurious and elegant, especially if you are attending a night event.

For the quirky ladies who simply do not want to join the multitude of women already wearing feathers and flowers on their hair, you can opt to use fruits and leaves instead. It instantly adds a fun factor to your entire outfit.

Clips, pins, combs, headband and elastic band

You will need something to secure your fascinator on your hair, such as the ones mentioned above. Using clips and pins is easy because it is just like wearing a barrette or bobby pin on your hair. Same thing for comb. However, these may not provide as much security as you need, especially if you have thin hair and if you are planning to wear the fascinator all day. For more security, you can use an elastic band which passes behind the ears and at the back of the neck. Headbands are also more secure because it is wrapped around the top part of your head. Ultimately, choosing which one you want to secure your fascinator with all depends on you and your needs.

Steaming equipment and iron

Some materials can be quite tricky to work with. They will roll up or wrinkle while you are trying to sew or create an ornament. What you need to straighten out these kinds of stubborn materials is to use a steamer or iron. There is a special steamer specifically used for millinery called 'jiffy steamer. You can also use an iron for pressing fabric and fine straws.

Miscellaneous

You might also need glue for attaching pieces together. However, keep in mind that glue is not often used by milliners because glue sometimes leave wet marks on the fabric and other thin materials, which makes the headpiece look like a craft project. This is why hand stitching is greatly encouraged in millinery craft. Besides, stitches are more secured than glue. Glue also tends to melt especially when exposed to the sun outdoors. You might also require pens, sharpeners, or erasers while working on projects.

You will need the following tools and materials if you are making a hat and not just a fascinator.

Hat blocks

These are like your molds for the different kind of hats that you are planning to make. These are a must-have for hat making, although not really required for making fascinators since fascinators do not really come with a hat. Hats need to fit the head of the person wearing it. And getting the right shape of the hat is not an easy task. People who make hat blocks are called block shapers, although there are only a few block shapers left because people no longer wear hats as much as before. Millinery enthusiasts look for those vintage hat blocks made of wood because they look more attractive than aluminum or poly blocks.

Hat stands

These are great for displaying your hat. You can place the hat on the stand so that the weight of the hat will not rest on the brim, which can lead to distortion. However, you need to consider the size of the hat stand. Make sure the stand is not pointy or you will end up with a pointy hat, which you do not really want unless you want your hat to have an awkward point on top. The hat stand should be rounded and not pointy.

Dolly

This is not just for displaying your hat. You can use the dolly while you are working on your hat. This makes it easier for you to add elements on your hat because you can just rotate the dolly so that you are facing the side of the hat that you want to work on. The main purpose of the dolly, however, is to have an idea how the hat will look like on an actual head.

The next chapter will give you some easy and simple DIY fascinator projects that you can try at home. They are ideal for beginners because of the simple materials and instructions.

Chapter 4:
DIY Fascinator Projects

Silk flower fascinator

This floral fascinator can be worn by the bride on her wedding day because the flowers are white, although they can also be used in other occasions. You can also make these using different colored flowers, whatever is available. Flower fascinators are always popular because they instantly give the outfit a feminine touch. This project will make use of silk flowers, which have been used by ladies from years before as decoration on their hair.

You will need:

- tiny silk flowers and leaves (choose two different types for this project)
- sheer organdy ribbon, one yard, 1.5 inches wide (although width depends on what you like)
- elastic hairband (choose something that matches your hair color)
- wool felt, small piece
- needle and thread
- scissors
- glass pearls, beads, or rhinestones (optional)

Steps:

1. Collect all the materials that you will need. You can buy the flowers, elastic hairband, felt, and the embellishments from any craft store. For the flowers, be sure to get them from the bushel or stem section instead of the wedding section even if you are making the fascinator for a wedding party because you will have more options there. The wedding aisle will usually just have something white and too formal, and the quality is usually not that good. Buying from the bushel or stem section will also

give you better looking leaves, and you need your leaves to look great. The flowers and the leaves do not necessarily need to come from one stem. So always be open with different possibilities when searching.

2. Once you have all the materials, you can now start deconstructing the flowers. To do this, just pull off the flowers from the stem, making sure that the petals remain intact. You also have to take off the green cup (sepal) that you can find under each flower. You can also get rid of the plastic that you can find at the center of each flower, although this step is optional. However, you should only do this when you start sewing the flowers because that plastic part holds the layers of petals in one flower together. You do not want to remove them all at the same time even before you sew the flowers or you will end up with a mess of petals.

3. You might run out of smaller flowers. If this happens, just use the bottom layers of the bigger flowers in your bushel. You will not need these bigger flowers, anyway.

4. After collecting all the flowers that you think you will need, you can now start

trimming the leaves off the stem. Be sure to cut enough leaves that you will need on your fascinator.

5. Get your wool felt and cut it to your desired shape, for instance, a circle. This will be the base of your fascinator and this is where you are going to attach all the flowers and leaves. If you are not confident about making a cut directly on the wool felt and you do not want to make any mistakes because you only have enough for one project, then you can make a pattern by drawing a circle on the wool felt with a tailor's chalk. You can then simply cut the pattern using your scissors. You need to make two pieces of the same size of circular felt.

6. Get your sheer organdy ribbon and fold it in a zigzag about 4 times. You need to attach this on the edge of the circular felt by sewing it on the wool felt. The ribbon does not necessarily need to cover the entire edge of the circular felt. This will only cover a small part. You can pin the ribbon using onto the wool felt so that you can sew more easily.

7. The next step is to start sewing the individual flowers onto the wool felt. Remove the plastic center before sewing each flower on the felt and replace it with a glass pearl, bead, or rhinestone. If you are going to use this for you wedding, the glass pearl is the best option. However, if the plastic center already looks pretty, then there is no need to replace it with something else. Just sew the flower right in the middle with the pearl also in the center. Better to run the thread through twice to make it more secure. Tie the thread at the back of the wool felt to secure the flower.

8. Continue sewing flowers and leaves onto the wool felt. Arrange them in such a way that the leaves are along the outer edges of the piece but try to put them in random places to make it look more natural. The flowers would also look more natural if the same sizes are not sewn together in one place. Be sure to cover the entire one side of the wool felt.

9. Once you are done sewing on the flowers and leaves, you should now sew the entire piece on the elastic hairband. To do this, place the hairband in position on the

wrong side of the wool felt, then place the other circular felt that you cut earlier to keep the unsightly stiches hidden, sandwiching the hairband in between.

You are now done with your floral fascinator. You can also add tulle or netting that will serve as a veil for a more dramatic effect. This is a nice touch especially if you are making a floral wedding fascinator.

Flower-shaped delicate feather fascinator

If you want something simple and understated yet elegant, you should definitely make this delicate feather fascinator for yourself. This is made from really fine feathers that are strategically arranged to form a flower shape. The key here is using the right kind of feather. Choose those feathers that are soft and fine and almost wispy especially if you are going after that ultra-feminine and delicate look. This can also be used by brides if you are using white feathers.

You will need:

- delicate feathers, which you can buy from any craft store for about $2 per pack of about 40 feathers, you will need about 10 pieces of feathers to make one fascinator
- comb or alligator clip
- felt, same color as the feathers
- one pretty button
- large needle or pin
- sewing needle and thread, same color as the feathers
- round styrofoam, or a cardboard box if you do not have one
- scissors
- hot glue gun

Steps:

1. Cut the felt fabric into a small circle. This will serve as the base of your flower-shaped feathers. Using scissors, cut a tiny hole or slit in the middle of the circle. This is where you are going to insert the loop of the button that you will be adding later.

2. Insert the large pin or needle into the tiny slit, and pin the circular felt on your styrofoam or cardboard box that is round in shape. This will serve as your guide for arranging the feathers into a circular floral pattern. If you do not have a circular shape that you can use as a guide, you can simply draw a circle on any work surface to ensure that your flower is a perfect circular shape. Pinning the felt onto the styrofoam keeps it stable and provides a flat surface that makes it easier for you to glue feathers. Moreover, the pin preserved the slit that you have created on the felt fabric.

3. Prepare the feathers. You might find those kinds of feathers that are fluffy on the bottom portion and fine and delicate on the upper portion. For this particular project, you need the upper delicate part that will serve as your flower's petals. Cut the part that you need. You can use the

fluffy bottom part of the feather in other projects so just keep them.

4. The petals should be uniform in size. To make sure that they all look the same, peel off the bottom layers of those feathers that are longer than the rest. If you want to create a fan-like shape for your petals, you can use your scissors to trim the sides of each feather.

5. Arrange the feathers on the styrofoam and around the pinned felt. Imagine the pin as the center of your flower. You do not need to glue anything just yet because you want to make sure that the petals of the flowers are arranged properly. You can still make changes with your petals during this stage. You can trim the stems off to ensure that the center is not too thick or you can add more petals if you want.

6. Once you are satisfied with how the feathers are arranged, you can now glue them on the felt fabric. To do this, place small dots of glue on the felt fabric, and carefully glue the feathers one by one. It is best to do it one at a time because the glue dries easily. You also do not want to put too much glue because you are working with delicate feathers and too much glue

may unsightly clumps of feathers. To give the flower more layers and texture, you can add plume feathers, making sure that the gaps between each feather are the same.

7. When the glue is already cool and dry, carefully pull out the pin from the felt. Get the pretty button that you will use as the center of the flower. You need the kind of button that has a shank at the back instead of holes. Insert the shank of the button into the slit where the pin has been. Using a small sewing needle and a length of thread, carefully sew the button at the back of the felt fabric to keep it secure.

8. Once you are done with the flower, you now need to attach it to a comb or alligator clip. Simply sew the felt fabric onto the clip or comb and voila! Your flower-shaped delicate feather fascinator is now finished!

Birdcage veil fascinator

This is another great alternative to the traditional veil worn by the bride at her wedding. You can also use this in formal parties and events for a dramatic look. A birdcage veil is just like a netting that partially covers your face. It is still comfortable even if it is in front of your face and can be easily worn the whole day. There are so many different kinds of birdcage veil fascinator. All you have to do is pick one that suits your needs and preferences.

You will need:

- netting or veil, about one yard (you can buy this at any fabric store or online)
- a cool decoration, like a floral ornament
- hat wire, about 1/3 of a yard (you can also use other types of wire as long as it is heavier than a chicken wire but lighter than a coat hanger)
- buckram fabric, or any stiff fabric (you can also sew two layers of canvas together)
- a comb

<u>Steps:</u>

1. For the flower ornament, you can either buy it from craft stores or you can make one yourself. You can also use other decoration such as a big bow or a bunch of feathers. If you have plenty of time and you want to make the flower ornament, you can check the instructions below.*

2. Get your buckram fabric that will serve as your mini hat base. Buckram is a sturdy fabric that is commonly used in millinery. Using your scissors, cut this in an oval shape. To retain the oval shape of the fabric, attach the fabric to a hat wire. The wire should follow the oval shape of the fabric. Attach the fabric to the wire by sewing it with a needle and thread. You can also use a sewing machine for this. The oval-shaped fabric will be placed on your head, so be sure to give it a little curve so that it fits nicely on your head.

3. The next step is attaching the comb to the underside of the base. To do this, just hand sew the comb onto the fabric.

4. For the veil, just fold it in half and using a fabric cutter, trim off both upper corners to make them rounded. Gather the

remaining corner by using a needle and thread. Do not pull the thread too tight. Give it a little room to do necessary adjustments later. Place the gathered edge of the veil on the top side of the oval base, the comb still underneath. Arrange the gathered part on the surface of the base evenly. Sew the veil onto the buckram fabric.

5. Get your flower decoration and place it on top of the buckram fabric where the veil is. The flower will then cover the entire base and also the gathered part of the veil. Just hand sew the flower decoration onto the base.

6. Ta-da! You now have a birdcage fascinator that will surely give your look a dramatic twist.

*Instruction for the flower decoration:

<u>You will need:</u>

- silk organza fabric (you can also use different kinds of fabrics such as tulle, china silk, silk taffeta, and so on as long as the fabric is lightweight)
- scissors
- a couple of feathers
- plastic stamen from plastic flowers

<u>Steps:</u>

1. Cut out 13 flower-shaped pieces from your organza fabric--4 small ones, 4 medium ones, 4 large ones, and 1 extra-large one. You can cut out flowers with pointy petals to make them look like water lilies. The petals do not really have to be uniform, but the general shape and style should look the similar. If you want your flowers to look like mums or puffs, you can make flowers with scalloped petals. If you just want something that looks like pompoms, you can just cut circular shapes.

2. Get the extra-large piece and mark the center using a tailor's chalk. This will be the base of the flower.

3. Get the 4 large pieces, fold each of them in 4, and sew to the center of the extra-large piece. Make sure that each of the folded large piece is on one quadrant of the base (imagine dividing the base flower into 4 quadrants). You will only need about 3 stitches per piece.

4. Once you are done with the large flowers, you can now proceed with the medium-sized flowers, still following the same steps in number 3. Just make sure that the medium-sized flowers cover the folds of the initial flowers. Sew the small flowers on top of the medium flowers, following the same steps as you did with the large and medium flowers.

5. Take the stamen off any cheap plastic flowers and insert these into the center of the of the flower. You can poke a hole through the center of the layered flower using an awl to make it easier to insert the stamen.

6. Sew the feathers under the flowers.

7. You can now use this as a decoration for your fascinator.

Glittery leaves fascinator

You probably have a lot of those floral glittery decors from different seasons and holidays such as Christmas and fall. If you do not want to use them every year as decor, why not repurpose them to something different, like a fascinator, maybe? You can use the petals of these glittery flowers as leaves to make your glittery leaves fascinator.

You will need:

- fake glittery flower or leaf decors from Christmas, fall, or other holidays and seasons

- tulle

- small comb

- thread and needle

- scissors

- hot glue

Steps:

1. Get your decor and remove the flowers and leaves from the stem using scissors. Try to choose leaves and petals with different

sizes and textures to make your fascinator look more interesting. It will not look as good if all your leaves look exactly the same.

2. Form the base of your fascinator by gluing three large leaves together. It is best to start with an odd number.

3. Add a few more layer of leaves, depending on how thick you want your fascinator to be. Just glue one layer on top of another, as if you are gluing playing cards together. One tip is to start with the largest leaves and then finish it off with the smallest leaves that you have. You can place it on the side of your head to check if you already like the size and the shape. If you are still not satisfied, you can keep adding more leaves.

4. Trim off excess stems that can cause discomfort while you are wearing the fascinator.

5. Attach the layers of leaves on a tulle. The tulle should be the same color as your leaves. If not, just try to choose something that complements the color of your leaves. To give your tulle a nice shape and not just leave it flat on your head, gather the long

edges and sew them together. Then, sew the corners together. You know have a nicely shaped tulle. Use a hot glue to attach the base of the leaves on top of the tulle.

6. Attach the comb to the leaves and tulle. All you need to do is hot glue the comb to the base.

7. You now have a glittery leaves fascinator! You can also bedazzle your fascinator with rhinestones, pearls, and other blings. Another option is to not add tulle--it would look just as pretty. To give you better control of the shape of the leaves, you can glue a circular floral wire on the underside where the leaves overlap. This allows you to lay the fascinator flat on your head more easily.

Vintage velvet bow fascinator

If you have always wanted to wear a huge bow just like Minnie Mouse, then this is your chance! But instead of wearing something childish that will make you look like a little girl, you can instead wear this DIY chic and stylish velvet bow fascinator. This is a timeless accessory that you can either wear with a fancy dress or with a casual pair of jeans and a t-shirt.

You will need:

- velvet fabric

- small comb

- fabric glue

- needle and thread

- ruler

- pen

- scissors

Steps:

1. Get your velvet fabric and cut three rectangular pieces in different sizes--5 inches length x 1.5 inches width, 16 inches

length x 4 inches width, and 12 inches length x 4 inches width. The sizes of the velvet fabric actually depends on your preference, on how big or small you want your bow to be.

2. Take the medium-length fabric (4 inches x 12 inches) and mark a dot on the center of each of the shorter sides (4 inches), about an inch away from the edge. Using your ruler and marker, draw a line from each corner of the fabric to the center dot. You now have two triangle shapes on both sides of your fabric, like what you see in ribbons. Follow the lines that you made and cut out the triangle shape.

3. Take the longest velvet fabric (4 inches x 16 inches) from the lot. Fold the fabric crosswise, making sure the two shorter sides meet in between, with about half an inch overlapping. Glue these overlapping parts to each other.

4. Lay the first piece of velvet fabric ribbon flat on any surface, then place the second fabric shaped like a tube on top of it, making sure that the glued part is underneath. Once you have finalized the position of the fabrics, glue them both together by adding hot glue right at the

center and also on both ends of the looped fabric.

5. You now need to form it to a bow shape. All you have to do is to scrunch up the center of the glued velvet pieces together. This will be the middle part of the bow. To hold the scrunched-up part in place, glue the folds together. Hold it tightly for a few seconds before releasing to ensure that the glue has completely dried up.

6. To make the bow more secure, tie the last and shortest piece of rectangular velvet fabric around the scrunched-up part. Glue the sides together, making sure that the glued part is on the underside of the bow.

7. Finally, attach the small comb on the underside of the bow by hand stitching.

8. Voila! Your big velvety ribbon is now complete. You can wear it with your vintage dress or to any casual outfit.

Birdcage fascinator with cushion and feathers

If you think you need to buy all the materials when making a fascinator, think again. You can use leftover materials from past projects because a fascinator does not really need a lot. And instead of just looking at your arts and crafts or sewing supplies, why not be adventurous and look around your kitchen? You might just find something that you can use for your fascinator. Such as a kitchen trivet, maybe?

You will need:

- a tiny kitchen trivet (just make sure that it is not greasy and dirty)
- felt or wool fabric (you need this for covering the trivet so make sure you have enough)
- batting
- netting (you can use tulle)
- hair fastener, like a barrette
- feathers, vintage buttons, or any other items you would like to decorate your fascinator with
- hot glue
- needle and thread

Steps:

1. The first thing that you need to do is to glue enough amount of batting onto your kitchen trivet. This will make it softer and puffier.

2. Lay your felt or wool fabric on any flat surface wrong side up. Place the trivet with the glued-on batting at the center of the fabric. The side of the trivet without the batting should be facing upward, and the batting should be touching the wrong side of the wool or felt fabric.

3. Fold the excess fabric upwards to completely cover the trivet. Glue the fabric on the trivet. It will look like a mess but it's alright because no one will see this part except you. But if you really want to keep it neat and clean. Just cut a small circle from the same wool or felt fabric that you are using and glue this over the messy part underneath the trivet. Glue the barrette or any hair fastener of your choice on this same side.

4. Sew the netting or tulle onto the top side of the headpiece, the side with cushion. Just sew one side of the tulle or netting on one end of the headpiece.

5. Cut a length of the wool or felt fabric, about an inch wide, and wrap it around the base of your headpiece using hot glue. The headpiece now resembles a tiny hat.

6. Now for the fun part, add as many embellishments and decorations as you like. Glue some feathers where the tulle was sewn on the fabric. Color of the feathers should match the color of the tulle. You can also glue vintage-looking buttons, doilies, lace, miniature birds, and so many other things! Let your creativity run wild.

7. Your fascinator is now ready to be worn to any formal event or costume party. You can wear a wool cape that matches the color of your fascinator for a more dramatic look.

Easy lacy fascinator

Are you looking for a fascinator project that is simple and easy to make but perfectly complements your vintage style? Look no more because this project is what you are looking for.

You will need:

- assorted lace, preferably about an inch wide
- felt fabric
- decorative buttons or pearls
- feathers
- hair clip
- needle and thread
- scissors
- hot glue

Steps:

1. Get your felt fabric and cut it into a small circle, about 2 inches in diameter. If you are not confident about your ability to cut a perfect circle directly on the fabric, you can use any circular object as a pattern.

2. Next, cut your lace fabric to about 18 inches long.

3. Do a basting stitch along one long side of the lace, making sure to tie only one end of the thread. You can do this either by hand or using a sewing machine. Pull the loose thread gently to make the lace bunch up, forming a flower shape. Tie the thread to secure the bunched-up lace.

4. Using your hot glue gun, attach the lace to the circular felt that you cut earlier.

5. If you want to make the lace flower look fuller, you can add another bunched-up lace on top of the one already glued to the felt fabric.

6. Once you are satisfied with the fullness of the lace flower, embellish the middle part with vintage buttons, pearls, or any other decorative items that you have on hand.

7. Glue several feathers on one side of the lace flower.

8. Finally, glue the hair clip or barrette after attaching the feathers.

9. This is a versatile project because you can use this for other purposes. Just remove the hair clip. You can use it as an accent piece to a bouquet of flowers or you can glue it to a vase or candle holder.

Giant flower fascinator

If you are the type of person who thinks that bigger is always better, then this fascinator is right up your alley. It is a statement piece not only because of its fun design but also because of its humongous size. And because of its large size, you would feel as if you are wearing a proper hat. You will surely get a lot of compliments because of this one.

You will need:

- 2 strips of fabric

- barrette or any hair clip, or headband

- needle and thread

- pins

- scissors

- iron

Steps:

1. Get your fabric and cut them into two strips. One is 45 inches length by 4 inches width and the other is 45 inches length by 5 inches width.

2. Fold both long sides of each fabric strip to a quarter of an inch and iron the folded edges down. Fold each strip lengthwise in half, then iron.

3. Take the thinner fabric strip and create a half knot on one end. This is where the flower will begin. Wrap the fabric around this knot to start. Roll and twist the fabric around the knot, until you reach the other end of the fabric. The rolls and twists will grow bigger and bigger as you near the end of the fabric. The twist that you are making with the fabric should just be a half twist and not a full twist. This will ensure that the fabric lays flat and can be rolled around itself to form the flower. Once you are done with the first fabric, temporarily secure the flower shape using pins.

4. Get your second, wider strip of fabric and follow the same steps that you did with the first fabric (see number 3).

5. Put the smaller flower on top of the bigger one, and hand sew them together. You can start at the middle since this is the most difficult and thicker part to sew. Make sure you run your thread through the folds and creases to ensure that the stitches are

hidden from view. The thread should also match the color of the fabric.

6. Finally, attach the barrettes on the underside of the huge flower. You might need more than one to keep this headpiece from falling of your head. You can also attach it to a wide headband if you like. You can also glue this huge flower on a beanie. This will surely make your winter outfit pop.

7. For a more interesting design, you can use printed fabric or two different colors of fabric. Since the size of the flower is already a statement in itself, there is no need to add embellishments, or it will look too much.

A cluster of pearl fascinator

Everyone loves pearls because they are timeless and elegant. Want to look instantly classy? Just wear a pearl accessory like earrings or necklace. This is why pearls are a popular material used for making fascinators. This fascinator project, for one, uses pearls as the main decorative feature. And the final outcome looks chic and stylish. Check out the instructions below.

You will need:

- a handful of pearls

- tulle

- felt

- silk flowers

- feathers

- feather boa

- flower ribbon

- plain headband

- glue

- scissors

Steps:

1. Cut a small square piece of felt. This will be the base of your fascinator that will hold all the decorative pieces together.

2. Get a square piece of tulle. Hold the tulle at the center and pull it slowly to form an imperfect cone shape. Fluff it to make it big and tall. Glue the tulle onto the square piece of felt.

3. Once the tulle is glued properly, arrange the other decorative items that you would like to add such as the cluster of pearls, feathers, feather boa, flower ribbons, silk flowers, and so on. It is best to arrange them to your desired position before gluing them all together. You do not want to remove the items after gluing them onto the base because this an damage other components of your headpiece and it might not look as neat. Be sure to glue the pearls in one cluster, because that's the whole point of this project, right?

4. Finally, attach the decorative piece to the headband. You can either glue the underside of the felt fabric onto the headband or you can also sew it using

needle and thread for a more secure headpiece.

5. Ta-da! Your pearl cluster fascinator is now finished. Go ahead and wear it with something fancy and be the belle of the ball, so to speak.

Steampunk fascinator hat

This is not technically a true fascinator because it features a hat but how can you not make this? It is so cool that it has to be included in this book. The combination of contrasting materials like pearls and tulle with leather makes this an interesting project to make, and a cool accessory to wear.

You will need:

- fake leather, preferably dark brown in color
- tulle
- decorative items such as feathers, pearls, buttons, organza, ribbons, flowers, watch parts, etc.
- a tiny hair comb and bobby pins to secure the hat on your head
- bias binding
- thin cardboard (you can use cardboard packaging or boxes)
- stapler
- hot glue
- scissors
- sewing machine

<u>Steps:</u>

1. The first thing you need to do is to draw a circle on the cardboard. The size of the circle will be the size of your hat, so be sure to determine your desired hat. You can use any circular object as a pattern if you cannot draw a perfect circle on the cardboard. It is okay if you have erasures because this will be covered by leather.

2. Next is to cut a circle out of your leather. The leather circle should be slightly bigger than the cardboard circle because this will be the cover. To ensure that it is slightly bigger, you can place the cardboard on top of the leather and draw a circle around the cardboard, making sure the leather is about an inch or so bigger.

3. Create a wide cone using your cardboard circle. To do this, you can cut a straight line from the edge of the circle to the middle point. Connect the two cut edges by stapling them together. You now have a cone-shaped cardboard piece.

4. You need to do the same thing with your leather circle. Cut a line from the edge to the middle point of the circular leather piece. Glue the leather on the cardboard.

Be sure to glue it tightly. You do not want the leather to have lumps and bumps. You want to keep it as smooth and even as possible.

5. Once the leather is glued, turn the hart over and you will see excess leather. You need to fold this into the cone. To do this, make cuts on the excess leather every few inches. This will create multiple flaps and will make it easier for you to glue the excess leather to the cone. Glue the flaps to the inside of the cone. You might want to use cloths-pins after gluing the flap to keep it in place while it is drying.

6. To keep the edges of the hat look more streamlined, you need to cover it with bias binding. You need to sew the bias binding around the base of your hat using a sewing machine. This can be a bit tricky because you are working on three different kinds of materials (e.g leather, cardboard, and bias binding) and also depending on the thickness of the leather. So be prepared to experience a little difficulty.

7. After the most difficult part, you can now start with the fun part. That is, gluing the decorative items on to your hat. Add the tulle, ribbons, buttons, organza, watch

parts, beads, and so on to one side of the hat. Choose the part where you cut the leather when you formed the cone. This way, the cut is hidden and only the smooth and uncut parts are showing. Be sure to position the decorative items before you start gluing to minimize mistakes. It is important to decorate only one side of the hat and not the entire hat because it will look too much if the entire hat has all the decors and blings.

8. First tip: You can make vintage looking flowers by cutting circles from your organza fabric and holding the edges over a candle to give them that old and wrinkled look. Just saw them all together one on top of another to form the layers of the flower and sew on beads at the center of the flower.

9. Second tip: The use of old watch parts gives this fascinator project that steampunk look. Just take any old watch apart and use the parts for this project.

10. Third tip: Use neutral colors for this project, like browns and beiges and blacks.

11. Have fun wearing your steampunk fascinator hat!

Paper medallion fascinator

This is a very simple and easy fascinator project and does not require any sewing because it is entirely made of paper! If you adore the look of those paper fans and you want to add them in your outfit, then this is something that you would definitely enjoy. This is also ideal for someone who is just starting to make fascinators because you only need three materials. You can also make this if you are in a hurry and you need something easy to make in just a short period of time.

You will need:

- 4 sheets of cardstock

- headband

- ribbon

- hot glue

Steps:

1. The first step is to make three paper medallions and one paper fan. To make the paper medallion, just fold one cardstock accordion-style, fold it in half, and glue the two ends together to form a medallion. You will need three different

sizes--8 inches, 4 inches, and 3 inches in diameter. To make the fan, fold the cardstock accordion-style, fold it in half, then glue only one end to each other, leaving the other end straight and unglued. The fan would look like half of a medallion. The size of the fan is 3 inches.

2. The largest medallion will serve as the base. Glue the two smaller medallions and the fan on top of the large medallion. The placement of the medallions and fan depends on you.

3. Prepare your hairband. If your hairband does not match the color of your cardstock, you can cover it with satin ribbon by wrapping it around the hairband.

4. Glue the paper medallions onto the side of the hairband.

5. This is only ideal for a single use because paper fascinators are not as sturdy as those made of fabric but at least you have something fancy to wear on your head on short notice.

Princess Beatrice-inspired fascinator

If you are one of the millions of people who watched the royal wedding of Prince William and Kate Middleton, you most likely remember Princess Beatrice, the cousin of Princes William and Harry, because of her fun and quirky fascinator, which was designed by one of the top milliners in the world. If you want to get that look, here is a DIY project that looks as interesting as what Princess Beatrice was wearing but definitely not as expensive. In fact, it will cost you next to nothing.

You will need:

- a piece of cardboard, 1-inch width by 16 inches length (to be able to bend it easily, be sure to cut it against the grain)

- a piece of cardstock, cut it into strips of 1 x 12 inches

- scissors

- hot glue

Steps:

1. To make the cardboard bend easily, roll it out first. Form an oval shape by bending the cardboard. Glue the overlapping ends together.

2. Get the card stock and cover the cardboard oval both inside and outside with cardstock. If you have time, you can paint the cardboard instead of simply covering it with paper. Just make sure the paint is the same color as the cardstock that you are going to use later.

3. Get two strips of cardstock and cut each into 8 inches long. Glue the two ends of each strip together, to form the loops of your bow. Glue this on top of the cardboard oval.

4. Get two strips of cardstock again, this time leaving the length as is (12 inches). Curl the strips to make them look like Princess Beatrice's fascinator. You can use scissors to do this. Just run the closed scissors firmly with your fingers along the cardstock strip. Glue one end of one strip under the left side of the bow, and one end of the other strip under the right side of the bow. You will not have two waves running

down from each side of the bow down the side of the cardboard oval secure the waves on the side of the cardboard with glue.

5. To better secure the bow and waves, get a strip of cardstock, about 4 inches in length, and wrap it around the middle of the bow and the top of the cardboard.

6. To put this on your head, just secure it with bobby pins.

7. You will surely look like Princess Beatrice when you wear this quirky fascinator!

Love letter fascinator

What better way to show your romantic side than to wear a love letter on your head? This fun and quirky fascinator will surely turn heads because it is unique. After all, not everyone wears a love letter on their head, or any other part of their body for that matter. You can wear this to a formal event or even to a book club or literary gathering. You can also wear this on a fancy date on Valentine's Day.

You will need:

- felt (gray, red, and white)
- lace
- barrette
- needle and thread
- cardboard
- hot glue
- scissors

Steps:

1. Draw a small circle on the cardboard, about 4 inches in diameter. You can use any circular object as a pattern. Cut out the shape using a pair of scissors.

2. Cut a slightly bigger circle from your gray felt. You are going to need this to cover the underside of the cardboard, that's why it has to be a little bigger. You do not want to have any cardboard peeking from behind the felt cover.

3. Using a needle and thread, sew along the inner seam of the lace ribbon. This will be used for gathering one side of the lace. Once the lace ribbon is gathered, it will form a circular shape. Glue the gathered ribbon on one side of the cardboard circle.

4. Next, make the love letter. You need to cut a small rectangle with a triangular flap on top from the white felt fabric. Fold the flap to make it look like an envelope. The envelope should be small enough to fit inside the circular lace. Then cut a small heart shape from the red felt. Glue the heart on the flap, as if it is the seal of the letter. When you are done, glue the

envelope with the heart seal in the middle of the lace.

5. You now need to cover the underside of the cardboard with your circular gray felt by simply gluing it on the cardboard. You now have a stack, with the envelope on top, then the lace, then the cardboard, and finally the gray felt.

6. The last step is to glue the barrette on the gray felt so that you can wear this pretty headpiece on your hair.

Mini hat fascinator

If you want to wear a hat but you do not want it to cover your entire head, why not wear a mini hat fascinator? The sole function of this is to improve your look and not to block sun rays because it is tiny. But it looks extremely cute when worn. As if you are a member of the Mad Hatter's tea party group in Alice in Wonderland.

You will need:

- a miniature plastic hat (you can usually buy these from the dollar store)
- black spray paint
- black glitter
- felt
- decorative items of your choice (you can choose ribbons, pearl strings, feathers, etc.)
- glue spray
- hot glue
- hair clip

Steps:

1. Spray paint your plastic hat with black paint. It is important to go outside and do this outdoors because this can get messy and also you do not want spray fumes

inside your house. It is best to apply two coats of paint so that the original color of the hat will be completely covered. It looks neater if the color is even all throughout. Of course, you can skip this step if your hat is already black in color. Leave it to dry outdoors for several hours.

2. Tip: If you cannot find these tiny hats from any store, you can always make one yourself using one of those disposable plastic cups. Just cut the cup according to your desired size, cut a large circle from a cardboard or paper stock for the brim, and attach the pieces together to form a tiny hat. Then spray paint your DIY hat. You can also simply cover it with black felt if you do not have black spray paint although this can be more difficult and tedious to do because of the irregular shape of the hat.

3. Take your painted hat inside and spray it all over with glue spray. Make sure that the paint has completely dried before you do this step. After spraying the hat with glue, cover it with fine glitter. It is best to use fine glitter for a neater and smoother look. You might need to apply double coating of glue and glitter to ensure that the hat is completely covered in glitter.

4. The next step is your favorite step--gluing all the accessories that you would want to have on your hat. For something simple, you can just tie a ribbon around the hat. You can also make a big black bow and glue it on the hat, then hot glue a cluster of pearls in the middle. But if you want a more dramatic and extravagant look, you can jazz it up with feathers, beads, pearls, and gems. You do not need to buy accessories for your hat. Just use the ones that you already have at home. You can use leftover materials from previous art and craft projects to save money.

5. TIP: If you buy a pack of hats, you can make several of these fascinators with different designs. You do not need to use all your accessories for making one fascinator.

6. These hats usually have an attached elastic so that you can wear it on your hair. You can also use hair clips or headbands. Just cut off the built-in elastic, glue a circle of felt under the hat, and attach the hair clip or headband on the felt.

Felt bow fascinator

Felt is a material often used in craft projects because they are easy to work with. You just need scissors and cut out your preferred design. They also come in a variety of colors. The texture of felt is another thing that makes people gravitate towards this material. It is just so luxurious to the touch, almost like velvet. If you want to feature this material in your project, you can check out the following steps and try to make a felt flower fascinator. This project also uses Cricut Explore to make the shapes that you will need to make a felt bow fascinator.

You will need:

- felt, 3 pieces in different colors

- interfacing

- Cricut Explore and Deep Cut Blade

- donut design

- bow design

- headband

- iron

- thread and needle

Steps:

1. Place the felt flat on an ironing board, then place the interfacing on top of the felt. The rough side of the interfacing should be touching the felt. Once they are placed on top of each other, iron them out carefully. Do this step to all three pieces of felt.

2. Get your Cricut Explore and pull up the template for cutting out bow shapes. The Cricut will then cut the felt according to this template. You need to use the bow template on two felt pieces.

3. Once the machine is finished cutting the template, you will have three pieces of felt that you need to assemble to make a bow. To assemble the pieces and to keep them together, put one on top of each other and stitch the middle part.

4. The next step is to pull up the donut template and use this for cutting out the last piece of felt. For the donut piece, you need to create pleats by simply making folds all around, making sure that the side with the interfacing is facing downwards. To ensure that the pleats remain formed, you have to stitch them one by one, iron them, or both.

5. You now have the two pieces for your fascinator--the bow and the pleated donut shape. You need to attach these two together by stitching the bow on top of the donut shape.

6. The last step is to simply stitch the fascinator to a headband so that you can wear it on your head. It is so easy and so fun to do yet looks so great that you might want to make fascinators in different shapes, designs, and colors using your Cricut machine and templates.

Vintage fascinator

If you are in love with those tiny fascinators worn by flappers back in the day, then you would definitely love making this project. Wearing this fascinator will make you feel like you just come directly from Hollywood in the 1920s! You can wear this at any formal parties or even as a part of your Halloween costume if you are going as a flapper.

You will need:

- felt, you can buy them in a pack at the craft store or or you can buy them off the bolt if you want higher quality felt
- tulle or netting
- trims, such as feathers, pearl strands, sequins, rhinestones, and anything that will make your fascinator look more fancy and glamorous
- pipe cleaners
- medium-weight interfacing, you can buy this off the bolt from any sewing supply store, this makes your fabric stiffer and it also hides the outline of the pipe cleaners which looks really unsightly
- glue

<u>Steps:</u>

1. Glue the interfacing onto the felt fabric to make it stiffer. The size depends on how big you want your fascinator to be. It is important to appply the glue thinly onto the interfacing because you want it to be as smooth and even as possible. You do not want a fascinator that has a lot of lumps and bumps. Put the together while the glue is still hot. Lay it flat on any surface and press it down with your palms.

2. You can now start drawing on the interfacing. For this project, you need to draw a hat shaped like a half sun. Just imagine drawing a sun and cutting it in two. That's how the hat base will look like. You can do this by drawing a half circle using a small plate or any other circular object that you can use as a template. Then draw rays around the curved part of the half circle. You can use the corner of your scrap felt to draw uniform rays. Using a pair of scissors, cut out the half-sun shape carefully. It is important that the interfacing is properly glued onto the felt fabric because they might get unglued after cutting them if there are lumps.

3. After you are done cutting the half-sun, you can now add trimmings of your choice all around the outline. You can use rhinestones, beads, sequins, or pearls. Anything that you like, really. Glue them one by one along the edges of the shape.

4. You can now attach the netting to the fascinator. But before you do, you should first fold the netting in half to make it a little thicker. Cut off the corners and make them rounded to form a semi-circle. Fold the circle in half again, making sure that the two straight sides are touching each other. At this point, the netting resembles a fortune cookie. Attach this to the middle part of the felt base. To hide the part where you glued the netting onto the felt hat base, you can create a small bow using velvet or ribbon and glue it to that part.

5. You want your vintage fascinator to follow the curve of your head. This is why you need to attach pipe cleaners on the underside and along the outline of your hat. Attaching pipe cleaners will make it stiffer yet more flexible. Add a couple of feathers here and there.

6. Blow dry the hat to remove any strands of hat glue.

7. Voila! Your vintage style fascinator is done!

Feather and flower fascinator

That alliteration alone will make you want to make this chic and stylish fascinator. The combination of feather and flower makes it a favorite among ladies who love to dress to impress. No need to spend $50 or even a hundred dollars to get a fascinator because you can make one yourself without spending more than $10. You can even make this without spending a buck because you can just use what you already have at home, like your left-over supplies from the first few projects that you already finished.

You will need:

- silk flowers
- feathers
- trimmings of your choice
- hair clip
- fabric

Steps:

1. Decide on the general shape and design of your fascinator. The combination of feathers and flowers can have so many different designs that deciding on it before you start working is a must. You can search

for designs online or you can come up with your original design. This project already have a specific design to follow but you can make some adjustments as you see fit.

2. Prepare the silk flowers. You do not really need to make a lot of preparations because the flowers are already shaped as, well, flowers. All you need to do is to add trimmings. For instance, you can jazz it up with a short string of pearls in the middle that will resemble stamens. If the flower has a blank space in the middle, you can make it more interesting by adding a pretty little button or a vintage coin.

3. Next is to add the feathers. Choose any feathers of your choice in terms of colors, length, and style. Glue them on the back side of the flower. You can glue the feathers in such a way that they are pointing upwards, forward, or towards the back.

4. Once you are done gluing the feathers to the flower, you now need to add the hair clip if the flower does not already have one attached to it. You are lucky if the flower already has a clip and some nice trimmings because it means you do not really need to do anything to make it look

a little prettier. You might also want to add a piece of fabric like felt or velvet on the underside of the flower before you add the clip to make it look neater.

5. Your feather and flower flapper fascinator is finished (more alliteration)!

Fascinator with hand-sewn flowers

One of the most important skills that you need to learn if you want to learn the art of millinery is sewing. And the good news is that you do not need to learn complicated stitches. As long as you can do basic stitches either by hand or sewing machine, you will be able to create projects that look professionally-made. Some people do not like gluing materials simply because they do not look as nice and neat as when you sew them on the base. If you can sew the material, then go ahead and do it instead of using glue because it will last much longer and look better.

You will need:

- fascinator base, preferably made of felt for that luxurious look
- velvet ribbon, about 25 cm in length
- plastic or fabric flowers of different colors, 6 pieces
- pretty buttons, 3 pieces
- hat elastic
- needle and thread
- pins
- tape measure
- scissors

Steps:

1. Lay the ribbon flat horizontally in front of you. Take your tape measure and measure 7 cm starting from the left end. Fold the right end upwards at a right angle. Fold this back down over itself. At this point, the right end of the ribbon is now pointing in your direction. The ribbon is now shaped like the letter L but the legs measure equally.

2. Get your base and place the L-shaped ribbon on top of the base. The corner where the two legs of the L meet should be in the middle of the base. Use a pin to keep the ribbon temporarily in place. Then start sewing. This is the part where you do not need to worry about making your stitches look neat because this will be covered later on by the flowers. You also do not need to worry about the stitches under the fascinator base because only you can see that part, before you put on the fascinator. But if you are the type of person who likes to do things perfectly even if you are the only one who knows or who can see it, then go ahead and make beautiful stitches. Whatever floats your boat.

3. Now start working on the flowers. You can use those plastic or fabric flowers that do not have anything in the center and are only one layered. If you are using this kind of flower, you can join two layers together by simply doing a cross stitch in the middle. It is easier to sew the layers together before sewing them on the base. Sew two layers of flowers together, giving you three double-layered flowers. You can also use those flowers that have many layers if you can find them.

4. Once the flowers are sewn, you can now position them on top of the fascinator base. You can put them in a triangular position that covers almost the entire fascinator base.

5. After deciding on the placement of the flowers, you can now sew them on the fascinator base. Start with the first flower. Place one of the buttons at the center of the flower, where your cross stitch is. Sew the button to the flower, then the flower to your desired position on the fascinator base. Run the thread through the button, flower, and fascinator base a number of times to ensure that it will not fall off. Do

the same thing with the second and third flowers.

6. Once the flowers are attached to the fascinator base, cut the ends of the ribbon to make it look more stylish. You will now have something that looks like one of those ribbons that they give out to people with awards.

7. You are nearly done. Now for the fun part, go in front of the mirror and try on try to place the fascinator at different positions on your head to know which looks best.

8. After identifying where and how you want to wear the fascinator, you can now attach the hat elastic. Simply put two pins on each side of the underside of the fascinator. The pins should be pointing towards each of your ears. This will be your guide on where you need to attach the hat elastic. Sew the hat elastic on the underside of the fascinator. The elastic will go under your hair at the back of your head. You can wear your hair down to keep the elastic hidden, or you can wear your hair up but be sure to put the fascinator on before fixing your hair to hide the elastic.

Long feathers fascinator

This project stands out from the others that also use feathers because of the length of the feathers that it requires. You need to choose a long feather that are about a foot long to make the fascinator look more dramatic. This will surely make people's head turn and you will surely look mysterious yet stylish. It also looks haute couture, as if it should be worn by people attending a red-carpet event.

You will need:

- long feathers, 3 pieces
- fake leaves
- trimmings
- hair comb
- pliers
- hot glue
- needle and thread
- scissors

1. The first thing that you need to do is to sew the feathers on the comb. The feathers should be right next to each other, as if you are sewing a long and narrow fan. The length of the feathers make them heavy so be sure to reinforce it with glue. You do not want the feathers falling off while you are at the party.

2. To hide the part where you sew the feathers onto the comb, you need to add a layer of fake leaves after the feather. You can sew or glue them on top of the feather.

3. After the leaves, you can now add trimmings of your choice. You can choose pearls for a more chic and classic look. If you want something that is really out there, you can choose something shiny and colorful, like rhinestones and gems. Anything will do but try not to add to many different kinds of trimmings or your fascinator will look too busy, especially with the long, big feathers. The feathers are already the centerpiece of your fascinator so there is really no need to add a lot more.

Eyelet flounce and shells headband fascinator

This is something different because it combines two materials that are not commonly used together in the same craft project. It looks sweet and innocent because of the light colors and the feminine materials used. This is something that you should wear if you are going after that innocent girl look.

You will need:

- eyelet flounce

- shells

- fake flowers

- head band

- needle and thread

- scissors

- hot glue

Steps:

1. Cut two lengths of the eyelet flounce. One piece should be about 8 inches long and the other about 6 inches long.

2. Fold the longer eyelet flounce first so that one end reaches the middle part. Sew this middle part.

3. Do step number two to the shorter eyelet flounce piece.

4. Layer the two folded eyelet materials one on top of the other. The shorter one should be at the top. The uneven lengths of the eyelet flounces will give the fascinator a more stylish look.

5. Add the trimmings. First, glue the sea shells near one end of the layered eyelet flounce. Next, glue the flowers at random places but near the sea shells. Try no to place them at uniform positions or the fascinator will look boring. You can even add one or two flowers on top of the sea shells.

6. Final step is to sew the eyelet flounce on one side of the headband. You can also use a comb if you do not want to wear a headband.

7. Your fascinator is finished!

Once you are done with all the projects in this chapter, you can now proceed to a more challenging project that brings you closer to making real hats. The steps and materials are a lot more difficult but they can help you prepare in case you really want to pursue hat making as a serious hobby.

Chapter 5:
Pill box fascinator using sinamay

This project is in a separate chapter because it is more complicated and uses millinery supplies for making hats. If you want to try making hats soon after you mastered making fascinators, then this can be a beginner project that you want to try. It requires more materials and steps than the previous projects in this book. After making all those fascinators, you are more than ready to tackle something a little more challenging, such as this pill box sinamay fascinator.

If you decide to make this project, you will need some of the hat making supplies that you do not really need when making the fascinators, such as a hat block and hat stand. You can borrow them from a friend who is into millinery. Or if you are planning to make hats in the future, it is advisable that you invest in these basic millinery supplies. You can buy most of these from regular grocery stores or craft supplies or anywhere that sells sewing supplies. Some materials, however, like the hat block, blocking pins, sinamay, millinery wire, and millinery stiffener can only be purchased from a millinery shop. You can also check online.

The use of water-based millinery stiffener for sinamay is optional. Use this only if you feel like you need your fascinator to have more structure. Sinamay is often already stiffened when you buy them from store so this part is completely depending on your preference.

It is also ideal to use two kinds of scissors because you will need a pair of scissors for cutting softer materials like threads and ribbons and another pair of scissors for cutting the sinamay which is stiffer than ordinary cloth fabric. This prevents damage to your scissor blades.

You will need:

- sinamay
- petersham ribbon
- hat block
- blocking stand
- cling film
- metal comb
- cutting pliers
- needle and thread
- millinery wire
- ruler and measuring tape
- blocking pins
- dressmaker's pins
- sticky tape
- tailor's chalk
- thimble
- scissors (for cutting thread and fabric and for cutting sinamay)

- iron

- bowl with water

- millinery stiffener, water-based

- brush

- apron

Steps:

1. *Preparing the sinamay*

The first thing you need to do is to prepare the sinamay. This may be a bit tricky if this is your first time to do this. You need to know the size of your hat block. For this project, you will need the hat block specifically used for making pill box fascinator, which measures at 12 cm in diameter and 4.5 cm tall. You will need 2 to 3 layers of sinamay. Two layers if you want a lighter and more transparent fascinator, and three layers if you want a sturdier and opaque fascinator. The size of each sinamay sheet should be 23 cm x 23 cm or 9 inches x 9 inches.

When cutting your sinamay sheets, keep in mind that one of them should be cut on the bias. What does cut on the bias mean? This is an important term in millinery that you need to know. To do this, you need to lay your sinamay flat on the table. Do this in such a way that the selvedges (or finished edges) are parallel with the edge of the table. Take the right corner at the bottom and bring it towards the upper left edge of the fabric, until the raw edge is directly over the selvedge farther from you. This forms a diagonal line. This is the bias. It is important to cut on the bias because this gives your sinamay stretch and flexibility, making it easier to work with. This allows you to roll the sinamay and is perfect for linings and trimmings. If the sinamay is not cut on the bias, it will appear static and bulky.

Aside from the square sheets of sinamay, you also need a strip that measures 16 cm x 75 cm or 6.5 inches x 29.5 inches. You will for your hat's trimming. You should also cut this on the bias. It is ideal to cut a longer strip than a shorter one to give you enough leeway in experimenting with the design of the trimming. You can always cut a longer strip but it is difficult to add to a short one. But for this specific project, the size mentioned above will be enough.

2. _Blocking the sinamay_

What makes sinamay a tricky material to work with is its texture. It is both stiff and coarse and turning it into a beautiful round shape can be a challenge especially if you are a beginner. But there is one key to making sinamay more pliable--water. That's right. Hat makers use water to make sinamay easier to handle. Don't worry about getting your sinamay a little wet because it will not get damaged. This a technique that has been tried and tested by expert milliners.

And since you are going to use water, you need to protect your hat block from getting wet. Keep in mind that your hat block is made of wood. And wood absorbs water. Water can damage the shape and form of the hat block so you need to protect it from getting soaked in water by covering it with plastic. You can use plastic cling wrap or any thin plastic bag that will easily take the shape of the hat block. It is ideal to wrap it with two layers of plastic to ensure that it will be safe all throughout the process.

Once your hat block is covered, you should now prepare the sinamay. Get a medium sized basin or a large bowl and fill it with water. Water should be at room temperature. Put your sinamay sheets into the bowl for a few seconds, until the all the sheets are wet. You have to make sure that all the areas are wet or these dry parts will be stiff. The sinamay should not be soaking wet but just moist enough to be handled. If you want the material to be stiff once it has dried out, you can add stiffener into the water. You may also want to use a waterproof apron while doing this to keep your clothes from getting wet. You want wet sinamay, not wet clothes.

Now the blocking process begins. Place one sheet of wet sinamay on the hat block. You have to block the sinamay sheets separately to ensure that they are smooth and even. Tug at the material gently from the sides, then pin the sides to keep it in place. You can use a thimble for pinning to protect your finges. Tugging at the sinamay will make it hug the hat block, thus preventing creases and lumps. You only need to use one pin for each side of the sheet.

Press on top of the hat block wrapped with sinamay sheet using your palm. Tug at one corner of the sheet with your other hand, then pin it underneath the hat block. You will have creases on the underside of the sinamay but this is okay as long as the top side is smooth and even. Do the same thing with the opposite corner, followed by the last two corners, until all the corners and sides are pinned.

The second sheet of sinamay that you have to block is the one that you cut on the bias. Place this on top of the first blocked sinamay. For this one, you have to pin the corners first. Just pull out the pins that you used for the first sheet then pin both layers together. However, do not unpin all at the same time. Just do this one by one according to which part of the sinamay you are currently working on. Follow the same blocking process as you did with the first sheet, except for this one, you have to start at the corners and you have to do some unpinning.

Once you are done blocking the second sheet, you can now get the third and final sheet and do the same steps as you did with the first sheet. You also have to start pinning the sides, then the corners.

The next step is to take the hat block out of the stand, flip it over, and add some more pins on the underside to ensure that the material is tightly wrapped around the hat block and that there are no lumps and creases on the surface.

Once you are sure that there are no air pockets whatsoever on the surface, you can now put the hat block back on the stand and leave the sinamay to dry. You can do this indoors for about a couple of hours if weather is hot. But if it is cool or humid, you will need longer time, from 12 to 24 hours. If it is a great day outside, you can always let it dry under the sun. Just keep in mind though that prolonged exposure to sunlight can cause the color to fade so be wary.

3. _Removing the hat from the hat block_

Once you are sure that all layers of the blocked sinamay are completely dry, you can now remove it from the hat block. To do this, you first need to carefully pull out all the blocking pins. Next, draw a line around the underside of the hat, about 2/3 inch or 1.5 to 2 cm from the edge. Cut off the excess material along this line using a special pair of scissors for cutting sinamay or straw. The underside of the hat block is now exposed. Carefully remove the hat base from the block. You have to do this slowly and gently or you might ruin the shape of the hat. This is another tricky process that takes practice to master and it is completely acceptable to make mistakes on your first try.

4. _Wiring the hat_

Now that the hat block is removed from the sinamay hat base, you can now add the millinery wire to retain the shape of the hat. You probably realized after aking out the hat block that the material can easily lose its form if not handled properly. This is why you need to add a millinery wire to the base of the hat to keep its shape and form. There are two kinds of wire you can use for this project--metal wire and plastic wire.

Whether you are using a metal wire or a plastic wire, you have to get the required length that you will need for wiring your hat. To do this, just measure the wire against the base of the hat block. Make it a little longer so that about 2.5 inches or 6 to 7 cm of the wire overlaps. Cut the wire using a millinery wire cutter. Again, it is important to use the right kind of cutter and not just your ordinary scissors.

To secure the circular shape of the wire, just wrap a sticky tape around the part that overlaps. The next step is to insert the wire into the sinamay hat base. Open the folded ends of the sinamay carefully and put the wire in position. You need to do things slowly and gently to keep both the shape of the wire and the hat intact. Sew the wire to the sinamay using a needle and thread. This requires hand stitching. Choose a thread that is the same color as your sinamay. You need to sew the wire all around to ensure that it stays in place.

5. *Lining the hat with petersham ribbon*

The main purpose of this step is to hide the raw edges of the sinamay where you cut it because it does not look good. Doing this gives your hat that neat and finished look. This may be on the inside part but you still want the inside to look nice and tidy even if you are the only one who can see it, right? You need to choose a ribbon that is the same color, or at least the same shade, as the sinamay. Temporarily secure it around the inner base part of the hat with pins. The ribbon should be a little away from the edge of the hat and the ends of the ribbon should overlap at about 5 cm. Using the same color thread that you used for sewing the wire onto the sinamay, sew the ribbon onto the hat.

6. *Trimming the sinamay hat*

You are finally done with the hardest parts of the whole process. This will be a walk in the park once you have finished the previous steps. You will need the sinamay ribbon or strip that you cut earlier. Place it on a flat surface because you will have some folding and pressing to do. Lay the whole ribbon flat on the surface and fold about 1/3 of one edge, which is about 2 inches or 5 cm. You can use your fingers for folding and pressing. Do the same thing to the other side of the ribbon. You will have three folded layers of the ribbon.

You might think you are done with using water but you are wrong because you still need it for the next step to make your sinamay more pliable. While you are pressing down on the sinamay ribbon, lightly spray it with very little water. Using your hands, hold down one end of the ribbon and pull the other end using your other hand. You are stretching the material to make it